RENAISSANCE NORMCORE

T0284525

Renaissance Normcore

Adèle Barclay

NIGHTWOOD EDITIONS

2019

Nightwood Editions
P.O. Box 1779
Gibsons, BC VON 1VO
Canada
www.nightwoodeditions.com

EDITOR: Amber McMillan
COVER DESIGN & TYPOGRAPHY: Carleton Wilson
COVER ARTWORK: Cate Webb

Canada

Canada Council   Conseil des Arts
for the Arts   du Canada

BRITISH COLUMBIA
ARTS COUNCIL
An agency of the Province of British Columbia

Nightwood Editions acknowledges the support of the Canada Council for the Arts, which last year invested $153 million to bring the arts to Canadians throughout the country.

Nous remercions le Conseil des arts du Canada de son soutien. L'an dernier, le Conseil a investi 153 millions de dollars pour mettre de l'art dans la vie des Canadiennes et des Canadiens de tout le pays.

We also gratefully acknowledge financial support from the Government of Canada and from the Province of British Columbia through the BC Arts Council and the Book Publishing Tax Credit.

This book has been produced on 100% post-consumer recycled, ancient-forest-free paper, processed chlorine-free and printed with vegetable-based dyes.

Printed and bound in Canada.

LIBRARY AND ARCHIVES CANADA CATALOGUING IN PUBLICATION

Title: Renaissance normcore / Adèle Barclay.
Names: Barclay, Adèle, author.
Description: Poems.
Identifiers: Canadiana (print) 20190089156 | Canadiana (ebook) 20190089180 |
ISBN 9780889713604 (softcover) | ISBN 9780889713611 (ebook)
Classification: LCC PS8603.A724 R46 2019 | DDC C811/.6—dc23

CONTENTS

— PART ONE —

— PART TWO —

— PART FIVE —

Hooray, hooray
I'm your silver lining
Hooray, hooray
but now I'm gold

—Jenny Lewis

Nothing wrong when a song ends in a minor key

—Fiona Apple

Part One

Part One

YOU DON'T HAVE TO CHOOSE BUT YOU DO

Would you rather be the sun or the moon?
Would you rather sing like Jenny Lewis
or Fiona Apple? I gave you a box from Lithuania
and inside it wind and rain. And beside it
space for another box. This isn't a nest
but a to-do list I vaguely mention
as if I know what I'm doing tomorrow.
The alarm will go off and I'll sink
into resignation that light isn't the ocean
but it almost is. I've replaced living
with swimming and reading Anaïs Nin.
I like when she shuts down Henry Miller
for correcting her English, trying to ply her
away from her diary. I read their letters
and imagine them both on Facebook Messenger—
all the dick pics he'd send; her, chatting up
several men at once and never recycling material.
Would you rather be blood or stone?
Would you rather receive or give a dick pic?
Be moved or be the one doing the moving?

Between us a storm
and two completely different skies.

WE ARE STUPID LITTLE ANIMALS

when I eat dirt
I look you in the eye
and I see you see me
eat dirt

and when I say a word
the sound waves
touch your face
and light up your brain

you twitch in a way
that says *okay*
and then I say *okay*

we take a breath
and jump into a kiddie pool
full of leaves and moss

it smells like plastic
and mould
this isn't a dream
you say *you deserve better*

as if I haven't heard that before
as if I haven't heard that before

from you,
you and your toy boat
lodged in the sink

I need to get out of this square
we built for feelings:
two floodlights pouring
into the sky

a text message, a supernova
or maybe a satellite,
the world or maybe
an avocado husk

I dropped my ring
beside your bed in the dark
you looked for it
and said, *oh no another poem*

HOW TO ENFORCE BOUNDARIES WITH PHYSICAL GEOGRAPHY

you packed condoms
forgot underwear
pulled your cock out
in the hotel hallway
and later wrote
to say you admire
my emotional vulnerability

Rebecca described you
as wiggly in the face
of seeing too much
uncertainty, she said
I see it too but somehow
manage to pluck
a way forward

and then there's the way
you remember everything
I've ever said, how you
register every gesture
I wonder if you remember
all the things you say
when we're fucking

Rebecca served me honey
cake for the Jewish New Year
in between my train
from Toronto to Montreal
and flight to Vancouver
my ideal is to touch
all three simultaneously

but it's Montreal
whose fever brushes
my cheeks, whose arms
hold me while I shake
in my skull
I left Sara and her black
cat in Toronto that morning

her mother worried
about her daughter's
indecision over which dish
to make for Rosh Hashanah
autumn knocks a dent
into her depression
that winter packs with ice

I've written to you like this
before, I had forgotten
some of the awful
moments like how
my anger turned you on,
the radius of your
free fall

you seem kinder now
age humbles as it dulls
we left the hotel
in the late afternoon
and I could feel a sweetness
rising in you, some sort of
flag unfurled

you ask for my favourite
Emily Dickinson poem
it's the one with mermaids
where the sea trespasses
her belt and bodice
she feels his silver heel
at her ankle

before withdrawing
he gives her a mighty look
I hope your students
like Emily Dickinson
I'm afraid of what days
actually look like
with you

not these nights
where we dive
into morning
I will say
the sweetness
felt hard
and earned

BURN IT ALL DOWN WITH WATER

I'd like to float on okay
but then I read about
the singer from Modest Mouse

I like to joke the upside
of an abusive father
is it teaches the absurd
tethers of obligation

love sometimes dwells
with violence, even though
that isn't really love
which is what Irene told me
when I was twenty-six

a revelation I haven't
fully internalized but live with,
a cell with a semi-permeable
membrane inside an organism
inside an ecosystem

I used to study biology
because my father
forbade me from pursuing
literature, moving to Montreal,
being gay, eventually

I accomplished all three
it's okay now
a lot of my poems
refer to salt, the only residue

THE FISH

Hunter says they've never
had their heart broken—
I didn't know I'm not supposed
to use *heart* in a poem—
I don't think that's something
to brag about

if all the queers of East Van
braided their hair together
we'd have to look
sexual tension in the eye

on a chart that roughly maps
the gender spectrum
I select *femme* and *dirtbag*
instead of *masc* and *dapper*

I wear a disco ball with wool
socks to the wrong party
no one looks at me all night
I cave and eat molasses
I cave and do push-ups

once when I was a kid
I lost my shit
because the story about the fish
whose tail went *swish*
came to an end
my dad told the story again
and then lost *his* shit
I don't know what came next

look, I just want to talk
and talk and for that talking
to feel like a lucid dream
or the heartiest fish
you've ever fried by a river

VICTORIAN QUARTET

When I told you I was a writer
you showed me your one poem
that spat kalamata pits

into the Mediterranean
like a thrifted Durrell in oxfords
wandering the twenty-first century

you took my photo on both coasts
I took your ghostliness
and mixed it into a muddy drink

a monk's offspring brined in a jar
its snarl tooth breaks the glass—
we've a curse on our hands

let's say there's a daughter
in the jar like a portrait on a desk,
that the brine reeks of coriander

this daughter in golden light
and dress brings you a rosemary
crown as your father drunkenly dons

a wolf pelt, your mother dreams
of a daughter to ask her ghostliness
questions, to count American bills

under the bed, maybe you're twins
and with your brother you're triplets
stuffed into a canvas pouch

then thrown in the gorge,
this daughter who is not a daughter
is a sister, is a spy who demands:

either tell the story four ways
or not at all

SUDDEN LANDSCAPE WITH INTERIOR JOY

God, falling in love
feels like waking too early
having to pee, gazing slack-jawed
at a tall landscape—

meaning lives there,
is urgent, almost depends on it

I swear I'll keep writing
for my tiny world with three towns
listed on its distance-to-next-
destination sign

some places feel closer to the sun
and they are

OPEN RELATIONSHIP WITH THE SUN

this woozy feeling
isn't jealousy
more like confusion
over time zones
and how it's snowing
in the mountains
as thirty-degree temperatures
smother the coast
bodies become bodies
unfurling for the sun
I miss you
and I'm thinking
of the ways I've fucked up
while missing someone
someone else
makes my bed these days
which clears space
to feel guilty about other things
it's been a challenging year
for my low self-esteem
still this innate
distrust of warmth
gathers heat

BORDERLINES

scraped by reef
I swim a choppy length
to prove something to someone

emerge stinging
on the shore like the flowers
in H.D.'s *Sea Garden*

Bryher rose from money
to keep H.D. afloat
cradled her mercurial islands

on Corfu they watched
a series of hallucinatory
pictures on a wall

I took my lover to Montreal
with inherited Aeroplan points
and left them by the river

I'm sorry that for our final act
I tried to analyze Justin Bieber's
video for "Sorry"

but enough about chick
and hare and our old town square
Pompeii has something to teach us

though after two hundred
pages of dissertation
I forget what

by the ocean I shed my skins
and steam with rain and swear
I'm going to learn about fire

IN A GROCERY STORE PARKING LOT

Fiona Apple cries while tucked
into the passenger seat of her father's car
when what she thought was a dove
turned out to be a plastic bag

I saved you half of this sandwich
and it became a carnival tent where your ribs
were the poles defining my fourth house
of home, family and personal foundations
I know it isn't fair, how do we
choose how we love

LIVE THROUGH THIS

Tori Amos taught me about the volcanic
goddess Pele and breakups. I carried
From the Choirgirl Hotel with me every day
in middle school. Even though I didn't have
a Discman, I'd pop it into the CD-ROM
of my workstation during Computer Lab
and listen with my older sister's headphones,
she wore Le Château black lace and clumpy
mascara, eternally Courtney Love in all her
bruised incarnations, sober-winged angel
moulting busted guts and gravel growls.

These days my sister and I convene easily
over a common enemy, but without trauma
as our anchor, the connection gets choppy.
I exit the bus to hear her voice more
clearly as it filters into the left earbud
of my broken headset. She is thirty-seven
and our parents want to lock her
in the basement with our mother's boxes
of undeveloped film. I advise *Take to the sky*
and *Tell yourself the house burnt down.*

SPELL FOR PISCES NEW MOON

I burn a floating candle in the backyard
for eclipse season, take three times
the recommended dose of vitamin D,
write *Arrivals are also departures,*
whatever that means. Neptune tells me
this fever is real and imaginary, paints
my dreams new colours: lilacs on fire,
percussive forest, blue that blushes,
pepper rose. Tonight Lana Del Rey and all
the witches will cast spells against Trump.
I'm not sure I want to bind my magic
to him or the snow smothering the Pacific
Northwest this winter. Yesterday
on the train, a man told me he could see
my pussy and that a porno shop across
from a school ain't right. In a Portland
bookstore full of white queers, I feel
the paradox of power and wonder if I have
the grace to rise, whatever that means.

CHORUS

Never underestimate my ability
to gaslight myself

DAMN RABBITS

what I wanted to say
became a jackrabbit
and the ravine
where its prints melt
into snow and mud
how can we shoulder
an entire season
what if the hollow feeling
is from too much fullness
the bone and gristle
that contain a love
before it assumes
another state
like the jackrabbit
from my last poem
about you
or the jackrabbit
I saw on my way
to meet you
how the ice melted
in my glass
when I thought about
whatever it was

Part Two

Part Two

FOR ARISS

I want to write you
so instead I'm reading
your grandmother's poetry

you emerge under streetlights
humming with your own
strength, Petra Müller writes
in "David's Hands"

the force of your left fist,
your reassurance I have
a resilient body

how can I say *Oh, this is only*
the beginning when this
is only the beginning?

RAINBOW ROCK-CLIMBING CLUB

I'm a gecko on a wall
that simulates a cliff
with rainbow grips
I'll touch any colour
that'll have me
midway is high enough
wary of emotional
cliff-jumping
I don't mean home-
steading like that queer
you overheard
at Turk's talking babies
after only a month
I mean relentless
breathlessness
forgetting to hydrate
having met at an awkward
sex party we now call a date
we walked for an hour
in the rain and talked
I've been calling you
the person I'm excited about
you thought I didn't
like you at first
I'm wary of a feral quality
I sometimes inhabit
Ryan called me
an *outdoor kitty*
I don't always know
what I think until I say it
and then I say it again

to commit it to memory
I'm afraid of what
you'll commit to memory
how you see my desire
when you're strangling me
I live with a lot of fear
that somehow
never really stops me

CARDINAL SIGNS JUST WANNA HAVE FUN

I can't sleep beside you yet

sometimes

you make a whining noise

velvet and leather
Cancer and Aries

my favourite sensation
is immersion in water
and this makes you
want to set me on fire
(literally)

after you fucked
the blood out of me
in your parents' bathtub
you said you felt
less stone

I slipped into
your T-shirt and bed
the pink full moon arrived
you took a photo
before cleaning
the mess

I want to eat all of the ocean

you are
fire, fire, earth

I am
water, water, air

you almost keeled over
when I mentioned my Scorpio
moon and Libra rising
I guess this has happened before

I'm relieved the house you invited
me to isn't your childhood home
because that has definitely
happened before

you have to fuck me
at least five times
before I'll flirt with you

PETIT BATTEMENT

is the difference
between dignity and grace
a shovel upon which to lean

it's been a while since
I've made myself throw up
and blamed it on binge drinking

I think life marks us
and sometimes I want to choose
the location of the scars

lately I've been climbing mountains
getting topped by nature

as a child you were barred
from playing sports with sticks

now you strike a match
against the night's boot sole
and I exhale stars

OPEN RELATIONSHIP WITH THE MOON

I don't want to live under the moon
but I'll stick its sickle and shadow
to my right thigh

when we met I bled fully
and now I haven't since I need
to balance magic and hormones

filling a blue jar with tap water
then pouring it out
onto the radishes in the yard

you see the Lovers splayed for Gemini
season and ask *when are we going
to talk about falling in love?*

each month brings new questions
as I settle into waves
that refuse to break into blood

SWEAT, WOMAN

My mother writes to tell me
she had a dream in which we swam
in a turquoise lake with orca whales.
There's a woman who wants
to leave my body through the skin.
At every sweaty turn she plots escape.
I lie in bed too late most mornings.
I carry faith in a bowl of milk
like a maid in a Vermeer painting.
I carry it down halls of white fluorescence
where the wives of wrong men
stand joyless. I seal an eggshell envelope
under the architrave with blood
wax, without ceremony, while awful
light scrambles in shadows. Open
your hands and give them a shake.

SELF-PORTRAIT OF 2018

a swarm of construction-paper bats
gather dust in an apartment
I moved out of in May
and now my mail gathers
at the foot of a stairwell crowded
with broken bikes, a drum set,
bar stools, garbage bags
of clothes, suitcases, an empty keg

when I lived there
I feared storing items
in the stairwell would kill us
if there were ever a fire
I finished a book and dissertation
from the top of that wobbly triplex
picked apples from a tree
in the backyard for breakfast

my ex had a baby
and moved to Paris for a month
I wonder if they got flustered
when their partner ordered
in French and if they remember
my mother's family lives there

I haven't seen my grandmother
in two years but my sister tells me
what spending time with her is like
how she mistook my sister for her
estranged husband and forbade her
from leaving the apartment after six

my sister visits the coast wedged
in a pit of a grief so big
it multiplies each year, we feed
the pit and ourselves fried fish
she tells me more of her story

the world is rattling as it always does
half my body dissociates and the other
half makes a pact with the ground
to gather resources for the storm
the storm that has been beating
its whole life into the ground

oh no thought we were done with these poems
I sealed them off in a book two years ago
during my Saturn return in Sagittarius

when I went on tour and read poems
addressed to you people asked *who's Sara?*
and joked *what does Sara have that I don't?*

I am taking a break from teaching first-year
university students how to write essays
so that I can write poems and go to therapy

which leads to introspection and crying
without the numbness of being busy
I am so open to everything that triggers me:

most interactions with men, alcohol
in my system, misplaced/lost items, irrefutable
evidence that my partner loves me, etc.

this afternoon is the blood moon
a lunar eclipse in Aquarius conjunct Mars
I was going to say Aquarius is alien to me

but you're a lunar Aquarian and I trust
your descriptions of emotionality even when
you ask me when companionship turns

to romance and I say it's up to the companions
eclipses are shadows planting seeds
the red light of Mars is harsh and kind

like patient impatience, a sigh signals *go on*
your bike gears squeak until they shift
and you ride down the hill, skirt lifted

it's gratifying to witness your Saturn return
in Capricorn as your passion and skills align
you left the art world and began writing

short stories and policy and it's like the lights
turned on in your attic home, the breeze
is finally cool enough to counter the heat

I am building a home with all the lights on
so that every joy, desire, fear can be examined
sometimes I am a sexy hole and sometimes

a sad hole, a soft ugly belly, tiny scratches
we call this slowing down and facing your shit
process, *soak and rinse*

when is intimacy not power, when does it sleep
when you napped beside your companion
was it a platonic or romantic sleep?

can you tell dreams what the boundaries are
when is karaoke intimacy and when is it power?
was it vulnerability that let me take a call

from my sister in front of you? this heat wave
and eclipse make me want to go to a matinee
and fall asleep in the theatre

Part Three

MELODRAMA/lust for life

The Little Mermaid
is best understood as lesbian D/s
Ariel gives herself to Ursula
willingly

I spent all summer broke
in shorteralls
and when Daddy stabbed
their left hand shucking oysters
with a stolen knife

I pulled them into the ocean
so they could slip
their right fist inside me

I WANNA GET BETTER

Turns out Jack Antonoff is partially responsible for a host
of songs I adore and it's hard work situating his baseball cap
'n' face in the airy background of my favourite anthems
that I routinely run to, a secret cleft tucked between treble
and bass, lodged under roots in the muddy woods Taylor
scampers through, ice, vines, wolves, lightning, fire—
he's there too. I'm no purist, I'm happy to sink into pleasure
without apology, I know his presence takes nothing away
from their art, how their voices make me feel seared
from the inside out, still it's unnerving like that time
during the witch's new year ritual when I wept
on the Maritime Labour Centre floor while my deceased
grandmother hushed me with a reminder: *There's so much
more—there's what you don't even know you don't know.*

THE STAKES ARE BELOW SEA LEVEL

submarine magma shapes earth stronger than smoke

sloshing like whiskey, you spit in my mouth

"She changed out of a leopard-print crop top and into a leopard-print button-up," is how my novel both begins and ends.

In the dream I ask my ex *Which one of you is pregnant?* My ex is swaddled in dark blue blankets so I can't tell. They hesitate, so I look up from the fishtail I am trying to braid with strips of stiff, shiny, grey cloth. They confirm that their partner is the one carrying the baby. A genderqueer friend has provided genetic material.

I learn from a Facebook post that in real life my ex and their partner are homeschooling the child and expecting a newborn. I remember walking with my ex on Dallas Road: they espoused anti-homeschooling views while I stared at the Olympic Mountains.

I've never had an asymmetrical haircut on purpose.

I want to reenact the webcam scene from *American Pie.* The girl undressing in the skeevy boy's room but this time aware of the camera. The absurd macho fantasy is that we're not aware.

I also dream a friend becomes a lover and informs me he is about to get involved with Gwen Stefani. He asks how I feel about that. I tell him it's complicated because I used to look up to her when she was in No Doubt but then I was turned off by her deep cultural appropriation of Harajuku girls. And more importantly I want to meet his wife.

I think I'm getting better at non-monogamy.

Your boss at the cobbling shop picks up a pair of mangled heels and hisses *Bad girl*. Later I'm reading my friend's crime-thriller novel aloud and a character pleads *Mommy*.

Both of these utterances give you feelings.

OPEN RELATIONSHIP WITH THE OCEAN

A pinhole projects the moon
topping the sun onto Portia's palm
she holds the solar eclipse
as it holds Monday
still we swim naked
for five hours in the ocean
without sunscreen

bare-handed
intimacy with a hungry tide
my skin's already burnt
when you mention
boiling all the cocks
before coming home

I am a bell
that won't stop ringing
until you dampen me with fists
a week later under the heat
wave's smoky pink eye
I line you up against the fence
and spray you with cold water
my hand closing over
the garden hose's mouth

EXPERIMENT IN DRUNK TWEETING

in love with the body of intimacy

what is vulnerability even

when we build this

how

I was thirteen and I collected a compendium of jokes about my middle-school teachers and emailed the manifesto to Lacey and Richard. I'd say the compilation was crowd-sourced but I still signed my name. The email spread like wildfire through fields of Hotmail accounts and I learned about how viral cruel pathways are, how they march directly to a school library's printers.

The vice-principal was leaning against the doorway of my sixty-student French immersion class. I hoped she was there to pull me away from a looming test and she did; she pulled me to the principal's office, printout of the nicknames and taunts in hand. They couldn't believe it was me, an affable straight-A student penning such mean-spirited jabs; surely it was the work of Owen who'd just been suspended for setting off fireworks in the parking lot.

The principal said what I'd written was *libel* and the teachers could sue me, a thirteen-year-old girl, for defamation. I was suspended and kicked off the Quebec trip; I had to apologize individually to each teacher and make a speech in front of the entire school about writing bad things on the internet.

When I apologized, one of my teachers threatened *If you were eighteen and male…* and then the principal cut him off. He had a black belt, he was the one who taught the girls self-defence. I had suggested that maybe he enjoyed teaching us self-defence a little too much. He made us spar with each other in front of him, he had me grip him in a head lock, he singled me out as an example of a timid girl who cast her eyes down which made me more likely to be raped. I wanted to tell him that really it was too late. He also singled me out as the best writer in the class; even after my transgression he would bitterly announce my superior writing skills and then complain about the new medication he was on because of the stress I'd caused him.

On the last day of grade eight I dropped a rotten pysanka egg that I hadn't had the chance to hollow out in art class because of my suspension on the carpet of his classroom floor. It was covered in colourful wax and full of awful yolk. He cleaned it up with paper towels and then took a picture of me and my friends on a disposable camera.

I TOOK THE 'A' TRAIN

I was delirious and dehydrated
from jetlag and a wedding
after the BnB host left for church
I went into the brownstone's living room
set aside the glasses on the bench
and played Adele's "Someone Like You"
on the piano. The action of the keys
was loose and comfortable
it was just me and dust and the ghosts
of jazz and gentrification
I remember piano recitals
in rural Ontario, a church or the one
art gallery where tiny white children
ambled through Billy Strayhorn's
"Take the 'A' Train" stripped of context
Bed-Stuy to Harlem—of course
my father, who played Billie Holiday
on the guitar, hated Bruce Springsteen.
As a teen my piano teacher and I
would skip our lessons to trauma bond.
When I was sixteen she told me
that with my upbringing, it was a miracle
I wasn't pregnant. I don't know exactly
what it means that I studied
the distant aura of a specific melody
through the molasses of decades.
The texture of draperies we wore
so thinly and the music kept us warm
though oblivious. I locked the door
and rolled my suitcase to the subway.

Part Four

Part III

PARK LIFE

for Brit Bachmann

Last night I sprained my right hand
taking a baseball bat to empty tin cans
of Park Life Passion Fruit Ale.
I smashed them until rock became
paper and flaked into the dry grass.

This is what ails the fruits of passion:
the child-sized bat casts a shadow
larger than itself in the fenceless arena.

Later: ice wrapped in cloth sheets
kicked to the floor, the sliding door inched
open, cats and raccoons hiss and trill
from either side of a rosemary bush,
a scraped slice of moon gives
imaginary depth to each act of night.

OPEN RELATIONSHIP WITH THE FIRE IN MY BODY
THAT KEEPS ME UP AT NIGHT

I unlearn trust like a sheet
sneaks off a corner of my bed
while my partner sleeps soundly

years ago I covered "Skinny Love"
on the piano and found a growl
deep in my throat as I sang
then who the hell was I?

the bridge between delusions
of grandeur and self-effacement
isn't patience or kindness
but something akin to a smoulder
that erupts into endorphins

when I feel the edges of a good
mood, when my body flushes
with generous flames,
when I throw a dart into the bull's
eye, when I hand you a knife
to carve a heart into my thigh

BLUE RASPBERRY

"What I know: when I met you, a blue rush began."
– Maggie Nelson

I pull a Tupperware of orange slices
out from under the bed for halftime
toss you a bottle of Cool Blue Raspberry Gatorade
your jock shows when you pound my cunt

There's a puddle of blood and cum
in the alley behind the community centre
if you're going to destroy my fishnets
please steal me some more from Shoppers—
size C or D—I've never met someone
so confident when shoplifting
yet so bashful about the size of their cock

I gave you a ring pop that turned your tongue blue
you looked like a little white boy
in a toque skulking down the Drive

What I'm learning: even Daddies have boundaries
and some babygirls lick until it burns

COYOTES HOWL WHILE CIRCLING THEIR PREY

I try to pierce your chest in a field
but I'm too slow and you're too tender

we hide our fucking from the horses
and the people who board them

at this medieval re-enactment farm
where we've accidently gone camping

with women who keep saying *women*
and tie rope around our wrists without asking

I feel less like a woman each time they utter
a hard *she* and more like a creature dancing

you look good standing against a red barn
somewhere there's a photo of you punching

my chest, coyotes howl while circling
their prey, scaring Fox who's covered in blood

when the shower cuts out you carry them
a pot of warm water, the healing circle never ends

under the heat we're not allowed to sit
women cry and fuck up a song

from *The Color Purple*, the bully tosses you
a ball of yarn and says *I don't know why*

there's just something special, she forgets
my name calling me your beautiful other half

I hurl a rock she gave me
emblazoned with *quiet* into the mud

WHAT COLOUR IS YOUR GRIEF

Oatmeal, blue, blood orange,
black hole, ochre—
I think grief radiates
has vibrations
and radio-like transmissions
definitely not *Definitely Not the Opera*
but staticky AM jazz
the Wi-Fi password
is *everywheretheresair*
the fanciest drink at the café
cooled to a sludge
like cornstarch slime
how it wiggles between
liquid and solid
in tiny warm hands

OBVIOUSLY A SHITTY DREAM

We're at your wedding to alcoholism
the invitation features
so many photos of your face framed by branches
I think you're getting married to a tree

I enter the banquet hall
and Vincent the emcee makes me change
into a stretchy fuchsia dress
gives me a lollipop

I'm sexy and chubby
he warns me Kim is here, skinny and off sugar

At the end of the reception
you weakly smile as you visit my table
tell me David was supposed to be your best man
but has been hard to reach lately

I wake up and think either
you got a girlfriend or are dying

INTIMACY HANGOVER

If I say a boundary out loud three times
does it make it real?

I CAN'T EXTRACT THE MEMORY FROM THE POEM

"Memory makes what it needs to make"
– Anne Carson

Rachel Leigh Cook teaches
a girl is prettier without glasses
and drugs are a rogue cast-iron pan
in the kitchen of our tender brains.

At nine I need glasses and don't tell anyone
for a year, meander up to the chalkboard
claiming there's too much glare
my father barrels through people
and walls and there's no one to tell
meanwhile girl power floods
the radio, the Spice Girls sing *Stop*
right now, Gwen Stefani's swimmer's arms
throttle the cover of *Tragic Kingdom*
I earn my Bronze Cross swimming
endless lengths to one day save lives
we practise CPR on a dummy as the pool
dampens the squeals and booms
of Aqua's "Barbie Girl."

At sixteen my father instructs me
to wear contacts and bikinis,
to highlight my dark hair, so I tell him
I've been bleeding for a year
and need to be taken to a doctor.

I CAN'T EXTRACT THE DREAM FROM THE POEM

on *Buffy* Angel murders Ms. Calendar in a dream
I resurrect her into a terrible half-life and decide
to bury my love for her in a poem
I send to some outpost of the internet
by mail I receive an offer of publication
in an anthology my parents identify as a scam
they worry about me writing about death
I explain the poem is about trips to the hospital
to see my sister who is suffering from a mysterious
stomach injury which shuts them up
I discover Sylvia Plath who reminds me of my mother
who writes poems and short stories in French
about the Acadian diaspora and islands of wild horses
metaphors for her abandonment and displacement
as a French Moroccan immigrant
she animates errands and chores in English
and French on a communal whiteboard
with doodles of the cat whereas my father
keeps a monthly agenda of serious ink scribbles
and lists with circles and underlines
one day I find chapters of his science fiction novel
on the family computer in a style that feels
very early twentieth-century exploratory Sir Arthur
Conan Doyle with Cold War anxiety set in South America
there's something about gold and the relationship
between scholarly adventurous men

I CAN'T EXTRACT THE MEAL FROM THE POEM

as a salesman
of industrial chemicals
for an American
company, my father
has an expense account
for clients, and because
of the exchange rate
he uses it to take us out
to Georgetown's local pub—
The George & Dragon—
where we devour
chicken wings and steak
and kidney pie
I watch my father
deliberate the draught list
before settling
on pint after pint
of Ricard's Red
he accuses me of always
choosing pop and chicken
fingers so for five years
I order cranberry juice
and a garden salad
which comes
in a deep-fried bowl

WORKING FROM HOME

"The body sequesters itself in a shuttered room"
– C.D. Wright, "Provinces"

The body hides in a shuttered poem
and on days when the sky is bright
the body calls you, its voice half an octave
higher than usual,

and on days when it's foggy,
the poem folds into itself, a tray for cinnamon
rolls, a cage for a rabbit, a rectangle
holding a wave that continuously rollicks.

The body only has time for Instagram sunsets
and breakfast, the poem styles itself
as a self-help memoir except the body forgot
to wake this morning, no one is listening

to its advice. In a poem, the body can imagine
all kinds of kin, in a poem the New York School
is never as far away as New York. The body
can walk through a gentrified neighbourhood

in any North American city and feel things
it can't resolve. The poem isn't transcendent—
the body merely mixed caffeine and nicotine
to complete a thought.

The body has quit smoking and most drugs,
and now plays with fear in a way the poem can't
always hold, but is beholden—to the body,
all bodies it can and cannot hold.

Part Five

WE ALL WANT MARSHMALLOWS

Katie, forest fires melt the air
half an hour from where you live
the sky is a black sheep bleating
and I can't even see the wolf in the photo
you texted me but I feel his snarl
in your voice over speaker phone

heat is an apex predator in a desert valley
I keep promising to visit and pick up
flats of peaches to can but Greyhound
cancelled its bus service in western Canada

you biked to the north end of Galiano
Island and a month later I followed
there were two coves to swim in
and one island to fuck on
our illegal fire by the water lasted
only minutes before a woman
walking her German shepherd
yelled *we all want marshmallows!*

we slept on a peninsula and I whimpered
all night because the voice that whispers
you're safe needed to let go
and when it did I felt my boundaries
dissolve into waves and wind

HOW MANY FEELINGS DO YOU FEEL IN A DAY

like you could quantify
a waterfall or a coffee mug
I'm over-caffeinated
and growing iridescent
scales as we speak
I blame winter even though
the days are sunny
and I'm lifting heavier weights
at the gym each week
I steal your dirtbag jacket
and grey toque to keep warm
and realize my Veronica-
Jughead hybridity
I don't have an excuse
for wanting to cry
when you vacuum
I'm a mutt with separation
anxiety and fear of loud noises
dishes are inherently violent
I know everyone's
got kitchen trauma
chopped onions
and undercooked meat
the manarchist
had a meltdown over
spoiled milk the morning
I finally broke up with him
yes it hurts to receive
I always start to feel jagged
and have to leave for weeks
let separation become desire

get drunk on the swing
from distant to intimate
until it smacks salt
off the rim of the good cups
we forget in the sink

PEACOCK AGAINST THE COLD EDIT OF REALITY TV

like Kathleen Hannah
on *The Price is Right*
the riot valley girl high-kicks
and leaves without a new washer/dryer

sad dog rolling on Astroturf
spectacle of the quotidian
its trickling matter
of cents—

I shoot modestly
and am thrilled when granted
the means to continue to pay rent
and Spotify

that is to live with pop music
so that the day-to-day feels less death-like
Lana Del Rey doesn't want to die
she wants to fuck time

and so we eat hearts
as they puncture our screens
we watch Antoni bring men
to eat avocados on *Queer Eye*

Jonathan talks about sun
and moon energies
and we think *maybe this one is queer*
as in *fuck you*

Once Michael called me *butch*
as I smoked a cigarette
in a green floral day dress and kitten heels
like a forties Presbyterian matriarch

I think he meant *queer*
or simply needed to negate
my femininity
to justify our intimacy

I've never had a tomboy phase
though I have a cock
and am sometimes called Daddy

mostly I am femme
mostly I want to receive praise
for my soft skin
that I'd invite you to touch
if it weren't for this screen

RUFUS SINGS THE GAY MESSIAH IS COMING

I was wearing a pink Rufus Wainwright
concert T-shirt that said *Better pray for your sins*
because the gay messiah is coming

I remember thinking *If I turn out to be gay*
this will be funny

Two years later he apologized for date-raping me
to this day he still sometimes posts
that Rufus song on Facebook

GARDENS OF ICE

"Ah ! comme la neige a neigé !
Ma vitre est un jardin de givre."
– Émile Nelligan

The sliding screen door of memory
too frozen to slip into lock.
My mother loves Émile Nelligan
something about his bilingualism,
insanity, tenderness creates a tether
for her to hold amidst these gardens
of ice far from where her mother
reads Verlaine and Rimbaud.
Gina and I drink a gallon of beer
and stumble through Carré Saint-Louis
to kiss Émile's indifferent bust.
A man corners us while we swim
on a bench and plays the Tragically
Hip's "Wheat Kings" on guitar
and so begins the awful summer rain.

OPEN RELATIONSHIP WITH THE EARTH

Luna says she's going to marry the earth
and walks into the forest alone with a basket

I'm drained from chanting and wiggling
my body in a cold field, all that meaningful
eye contact with strangers, rituals that command
me to grieve for the earth and all the animals

I think maybe I'm a witch who prefers
to sing Ariana Grande, who reads Francesca
Lia Block and then dives into a lake,
who accidentally drops the Tower, the Star
and Queen of Pentacles
between the boards of the dock

I can't speak for the lake the mountain,
the glacier, but I can talk about astrological
compatibility and purple lipstick

everyone keeps shouting that
everything is connected and I feel it
but telling me to feel it only makes it feel awful

Luna returns with a pentacle on her forehead
and the prettiest smile

FLOAT SICKNESS

I am sick of Anne Carson
I read her every week
I mean I love her, she's brilliant
her poems so jaunty yet precise
it takes all my graduate degrees
and intuition to follow her
stacks, clips and drops
I read her and knew I couldn't
fall in love with her—
every "fuck" placed too well
meanwhile I ran a quarter of the way
to the citadel and then gave up
I'm miffed because I was told
she's a lesbian but she isn't
I thought her shame was
my shame but then it wasn't

Björk is Icelandic though she was teased
and called *China girl* as a child
the night before second year
someone in cognitive sciences said
you look like Björk as I wandered off
drunk as a comet

another night at the Greek Club's toga party
with a chorus of six roommates
a Lebanese guy followed me around all evening
telling me I was Lebanese when all I needed
was to puke while draped in a white sheet
he didn't believe my explanation *I'm French!*
with hair pulled back in two French braids
care of Natalie maybe before she hated me
Charlotte blacked out and somehow
we sailed our drunken vessel home

I can barely remember that night and others
I can barely braid my own hair, arms pressed
tight to the body, stiff little devil

I didn't make you
I didn't make you
I did

SURPRISE PARTIES REQUIRE GASLIGHTING

I consent to surprises, certain nothing could truly
surprise me though I startle easily, I jump and giggle
uncontrollably like my friend in grade school
who'd laugh while being bullied. Surprise parties
require gaslighting, they're a form of devoted aggression,
I even gaslit myself to serve the surprise birthday
ignoring texts about hiding spots and the resurrection

of Elaine's opulent wedding dress. Somehow despite
the obvious, the takedown occurred as a revelation,
they carted me by limb and hair across the room.
In *Jawbreaker* from 1999, a clique of girls kidnap
their friend for her birthday and accidentally murder her
by shoving a jawbreaker in her mouth, then Rose
McGowan's character fucks a stranger—a cameo

by Marilyn Manson—in her friend's bed to circumvent
responsibility for her death. I like the film's reversal
of stranger danger, how easily culpability is deferred
to a random when really the violence is far more
intimate and sisterly, it's like a bubble-gum filtered
and more efficient *Twin Peaks* where we blame
the evil demon Bob but we know it's really the father

committing all those acts of rape and murder.
Ghost stories draw our attention to fear and grief
without pining them to the earth. In horror movies,
humans are hapless at best and careless at worst,
rarely accountable. How do we trudge through
hallways and elevators of blood and celebrate
a surprise party where ghosts tend to the gaslights.

OUR BEAUTY WAS LOST TO THE ALGORITHM

January 16, 2019: after Mary Oliver a day before her death

I am trying to survive
each time the word *family* comes up
in conversation
please let's just talk about tarot
and our pets

Nadia's cat casts a spell
to woo raccoons
wanting what we don't want her to want
she is a Scorpio after all

Cricket was born
the day we met
which makes me both hopeful
and wary of time
how we now count
our connection by her life

I could boast about our beauty
but it's lost to the algorithm
when others want you
they don't see you
reading to me
to get me to fall asleep

soft creatures awake all night
here is a playlist of thunderstorms
a book I really loved
a shiny rock
a recipe for anger
that won't self-destruct

I don't know what to do
with all that lives inside of living
in the corner of the apartment
we find Cricket's latest toy
a hazelnut

MOONS CAN HAVE MOONS AND THEY ARE CALLED MOONMOONS

call me whatever orbits
your moon, your moon's moon
light doesn't always make light
sometimes it brightens and dies

the moonmoon is weary
with feeling and waning
when the moon is full
like how I track
your menstrual cycle and say
it'll come on Wednesday
because mine was supposed
to come on Monday

Tillie and I determine West
is a power bottom, North is thud
she slices her finger offering me
obsidian and South is blood

I select a piece of volcanic glass
with a thick grip, mostly dull
and only one sharp point
she warns me not to cut you
with it unless you want me to

HOW DO YOU RESPOND TO CONFLICT

like I've stumbled across a bear
I can't imagine throwing things by the river
I make a fist and water evaporates into stars
that shoot a sad missive against the current

I want a fixed spot around which
to tetherball my needs

lions signal fidelity but trauma
braces like a tiger's dead stare

last May in parc Laurier
Klara and I made a caffeinated blood pact
to dedicate our lives to poetry

chucked everything else
into the Saint Lawrence and my stomach
conducted electricity—
either I found my limits or my cruelty

"The Fish" takes its title from Elizabeth Bishop's poem of the same name.

"Live Through This" takes its title from Hole's album of the same name.

"How to Enforce Boundaries with Physical Geography" makes use of lines from Emily Dickinson's "I started Early – Took my Dog (656)" and Gwendolyn MacEwen's "Daynights."

"Borderlines" takes its title from the film *Borderline* directed by Kenneth Macpherson and produced by the Pool Group, Macpherson, H.D. and Bryher. The seventh stanza of "Borderlines" makes use of lines from H.D.'s *Trilogy*.

"Victorian Quartet" references Lawrence Durrell's *The Alexandrian Quartet* in its title and a few lines.

"Sudden Landscape with Interior Joy" takes its title from Brenda Shaughnessy's *Interior with Sudden Joy*.

"In a Grocery Store Parking Lot" references Fiona Apple's song "Paper Bag."

"MELODRAMA/lust for life" takes its title from Lorde's album *Melodrama* and Lana Del Rey's album *Lust for Life*.

"I Wanna Get Better" takes its title from the Bleachers' song of the same name.

"Moons Can Have Moons and They Are Called Moonmoons" takes its title from a headline from *NewScientist*.

"Sometimes a Constellation Is Just a Drunk Comet" relies on biographical information from *Björk: Wow & Flutter* by Mark Pytlik.

ACKNOWLEDGEMENTS

My sincere thanks to the editors of the publications in which these poems, in earlier versions, appeared:

PRISM international: "Sweat, Woman"

glitterMOB: "We Are Stupid Little Animals" and "Bad Women"

Vallum: "Obviously A Shitty Dream"

Heavy Feather Review: "Rainbow Rock-Climbing Club"

Room Magazine: "Open Relationship with The Ocean," "Open Relationship with The Moon," and "Borderlines"

Hart House Review: "Sudden Landscape with Interior Joy"

The Malahat: "For Ariss"

Eighteen Bridges: "Self-Portrait of 2018"

Cascadia Magazine: "We All Want Marshmallows"

ALPHA: "Burn It All Down with Water" and "How Do You Respond to Conflict"

Fog Machine: "You Don't Have to Choose but You Do"

I am grateful to the Canada Council of the Arts and *Arc Magazine*'s Poet in Residence program for the time and financial assistance crucial to the completion of this book.

Thank you to the Banff Centre for the Arts and Creativity for accepting me into the 2017 Writing Studio and especially to Karen Solie and Ocean Vuong for their guidance as I began writing these poems. And thank you to Hoa Nguyen whose Anne Carson/Sappho translations course conjured a few of these poems.

This book owes its improved existence to Amber McMillan whose keen heart and foresight made these poems feel possible. I am grateful to Silas White, Marisa Alps, and the whole Nightwood and Harbour crews for their true expertise and dedication.

Thank you to Cate Webb for the gorgeous cover illustration and Carleton Wilson for designing the book of my dreams.

For conversation, feedback, curiosity, my fellow conspirators: Rebecca Rustin, Jake Byrne, Sara Fruchtman, Mallory Tater, Curtis LeBlanc, Shaun Robinson, Selina Boan, Kyla Jamieson, Leah Horlick, Amber Dawn, Erin Flegg, Brit Bachmann, Justine Little, Katie Harris, Nadia Grutter and Klara Du Plessis. Thank you to Kayla Czaga for playfully bouncing around the term "Renaissance Normcore" with me while discussing sartorial styles.

To my family, especially my dear sister Elissa Barclay.

Thank you to Ariss Grutter for love and light.

ABOUT THE AUTHOR

Adèle Barclay is the author of *If I Were in a Cage I'd Reach Out for You*, which won the 2017 Dorothy Livesay Poetry Prize. She is the recipient of the 2016 Lit POP Award for Poetry and *The Walrus'* 2016 Readers' Choice Award for Poetry and has been nominated for a Pushcart Prize. Her poems have appeared in *Vallum, Cosmonauts Avenue, Room Magazine, The Puritan, Heavy Feather Review, glitter-MOB, The Fiddlehead* and elsewhere.

She is *Arc Magazine's* 2018–19 Poet in Residence and an editor at Rahila's Ghost Press. She lives on the unceded territories of the Squamish, Tsleil-Waututh and Musqueam First Nations.

PHOTO CREDIT: ERIN FLEGG